Painting Trees

Painting Trees

Naomi Myles

BOSON BOOKS
Raleigh, NC

Naomi Myles was born in New York City and has lived in Charlotte, North Carolina, since 1956. She is a graduate of Goddard College in Vermont. Her commitment to poetry follows a career as a free-lance writer and journalist. She is a member of the North Carolina Writers Network and the North Carolina Poetry Society.

Some of these poems have appeared in the *Arts Journal, Black Buzzard Review, Calliope, Charlotte Poetry Review, Pembroke Magazine*, and *Potato Eyes*.

Published by **Boson Books**
An imprint of C&M Online Media, Inc.
3905 Meadow Field Lane,
Raleigh, NC 27606-4470
cm@cmonline.com

http://www.bosonbooks.com

ISBN (paper): 1-932482-01-6
ISBN (ebook): 1-886420-57-2

Cover silkscreen print "Tree #2" by Jean Myles Eger

Contents

Painting Trees
...From *The Mustard Seed Manual of Painting*

The first thing to avoid
Jao Tzu-jan said
is a crowded, ill-arranged
composition.
Always aim for clarity.
Distinguish far and near
and be sure to indicate
the source of water.

Old trees are like hermits
whose purity shows
in their appearance.
Those which have clung to steep cliffs
for many years
are lean and gnarled
and their bones protrude.

Jao says it is good to vary
the pattern: Let some roots
be hidden and some exposed,
for if all roots are shown
They will look like
the teeth of a saw.

When Everything is Possible

In the cleft of the seasons
just when winter ends
the shoulder of the mountain
wears winter white.
Unannounced
the wild young iris push upward,
forsythia waves its careless branches,
the sweet sharp wind
sweeps up the valley
tempts fate
taking bets
on an early spring.

Home Place

When I climbed the big tree stump
looked over waist-high weeds
past saplings and cornfield
to where the mountain scored
the far horizon

I heard whisperings,
watched clouds drawn in great rhythms
west to east,
saw fierce sunset pink
beyond the western ridge.

Then I staked the corners
of my house between oak and hickory;
the heap of old chimney stone
and tangle of roses
placed history
squarely on my side.

It was like walking the rough earth
with a dowser,
waiting for the willow
fork to twist my fist
earthward, insisting
I dig here.

In the Shadow of the Groundhog

The groundhog in my life lives quietly
just below the hill. A big one, this Monax,
who feasts on my garden crop while I watch.
Its glossy gray coat catches a glint of sun
cooling to its end as shadows lengthen
over raspberries and roses and the line
of mountain crests melts over the horizon
like a mirage. Known to the Indians as "wejack"
or "etchig" Monax is a minor sort of
bear-like creature who devotes itself
to keeping its incisors trim with constant
gnawing, which is pretty much what we all
do who live in burrows, quietly.

On Greening

The ant that scurries at my feet
commands no reason.
It merely is; carries on its back
a complex history much as my own.

All are swept by the wind
by earth's turning
the shape of trees.

Sagan says life is warfare
and man's body as the coursing waters,
a brief sojourn in an alien land.

So I count myself lucky
to concentrate on greening
my small patch of garden,
barring the accidental thrust
of a giant foot.

To an Unknown Species

First to flower, the odd willow
outside my window welcomes Spring
its leaves reluctant
to brave the winds of March.

Budding, it grows plumply
swelling and swelling
till the fragile pink petals
open, quivering in the breeze.

And still no leaves — neither
book nor botanist willing to say
for sure: Wild plum. French willow.
Some Oriental variety of salix.

It is like my uncertainty,
puzzling over my own young
as they blossom into puberty
and me at a loss to name it.

Smart Cat

My neighbor's mouser
knows a good thing
when she sees it.
The shed out back
suits her purpose
and she means to make
the most of it.
Sometimes
she slips into the dark
where no one can reach her
beds down in the dust
among the cast-offs
seeking aloneness
that sweet dream state
where no one
asks questions
or raps out orders.
She knows
it's easier to find peace
at the neighbor's house
than face the music at home.

Dream Mountain

Cruising the old drover's track
north from Asheville
my car on automatic pilot
radials caressing the rough skin of road

I brood upon the ancient ones
whose footsteps repeated the rhythms
of these peaks before the Iron Age arrived
speaking Spanish.

Dim among the giant trees
I see Cherokees, hunters of bear,
the old gods lingering
in the curves of the road,

clinging to these mountains
like the stubborn pioneer settlers
who prodded their docile flocks
to market here, straining against

the thrust of stone and rubble
my car overcomes with ease
as though ordained. And with
the land shifting and blurring on either side

did they see, as I do now,
looming up before them in the distance
an air-borne mountain with snow on its flanks
aloof, indifferent, self-absorbed?

Did it light the way home for them?

Was it reward enough?

Trade-Off

They've planted a chain-link fence
around the home place
to hold back the wilderness.

It shuts out the view
of Seven Mile Ridge
and the Black Mountain Range
that once merged for me
on the far horizon.

I think of the groundhog
who lived below the hill
and wonder whose garden
he sharpens his long canines on.

Along the path to blackberries
where rangers in helicopters
dropped seedlings
pale clones of pine rise
like ghosts from the scummy water
of the strip mine pit
whose sour green deep
once glared at me.

I count my losses
turn my footsteps homeward
console myself with blackberries.

Small Stuff

Cherish all things
small and tender:
birds winging it,
quicksilver squirrels,
sea creatures
jewelled lizards,
mice.
They nest in crevices
between leaf and branch,
burrow in secret places,
their necessary homes,
precise and vital
as yours and mine.

Orchids

...more from *The Mustard Seed Manual of Painting*

In painting orchids
the fellow painter
Li Shan advised
one should proceed from leaves to petals
single stems to bunches.

With leaves orderliness prevails,
the hand moves from left to right
and then counterstroke,
right to left.

They must float with the wind
veiling the flowers
yet supporting them.

Draw from roots up
so that blossoms appear
wrapped in leaves
each in its position and angle.

Thus stems are straight and erect
and the flowers are heavy.
And within the heart of the orchid
is a three-dotted stamen.

And if some orchids are in bud
and others full bloom,
the mood is a happy one.

Maps

If I start at the top of the world
it all comes back.
A long country road I drove
with someone I loved.
I could do it again with my eyes closed.

A map stops time in its tracks
as if what happened then is happening right now.
It will lay things out for you plain as day,
clear as your mother's voice
telling right and wrong,
pointing the way to go.

There are no clouds in the sky of a map.
A palmist would find no shadows
on the familiar lines of your hand.
Even the dream you dreamt last night
that mapped the topography of your desire
was cloudless.

Lucretius

Merely a poet to the Romans
but to me in my youth
his mooned sands, eternal drift,
seemed right on target.

He promoted the atom, building block
of nature, sent it spinning
through space, part of the eternal
drift, the flow.
Struck down shadows on the walls
of caves, worship of things
unseen, celebrated the thing
itself: round, angular, soft,
brittle, dry, warm,
sent them on to penetrate the heavens
puzzle their way to quantum
and the primal source.

All things flow, he said,
nothing is born of nothing.
And since poets are soon forgotten
the centuries passed him by.
Somehow, his words lived on.

From the Pages of the Geographic

You feel the bulge and curve of stone
mostly at night when soft things
wrap themselves around you
and take you back to the first
room's warmth and light.
Like the caves you see in the pages
of the Geographic,
light filtering down tunnels
in Morocco or the Sudan
or the curving rough walls
of cliff dwellings along the Loire
trimmed with wood and plaster
and grainy to the touch.
Think of those muscled sinewy
chambers resonating backwards
rank upon rank of them
nourished by quarried piers
living walls of stone.

Looking for Bensonhurst

Odd, isn't it, how some people like
to drive the blue roads, avoid throughways,
while others like the red roads,
everything laid out for them
speed limits and all.

Blue or red, it's Russian Roulette
out there, bumper-to-bumper
with mad men on their way to a six-pack
and maybe a gun in the side pocket.

But either way a map is called for
though even a good map won't tell
what they need to know.

And somehow they blunder through
like the man Thomas Wolfe told about
who asked the way to Bensonhurst
just because he liked the sound of it
and found he'd need to navigate
the Brooklyn subway, and that would take
a lifetime.

He, being a blue man, simply had to try
because he loved the purr of a motor,
a road unraveling ahead.
and he wanted to look at Bensonhurst,
wherever that is.

Brouhaha!

For the sake of science
   she lived in a cave
      for 111 days
walled in by liquid rope
   descending on itself
      and stretching down
to the cold wet floor
   275 feet underground
      darkness unfurling
against a barren shield of stone.
   Cultivation in this situation
      meant hoeing and seeding
a hedge of instruments
   to measure her body's
      rage and her mind's
rebellion while coping
   with sober thoughts
      of good and evil -
oddly intoxicating
   in a scientific way -
      though it didn't seem
to matter when all she could grasp
   was the sound of her heart
      and the faint murmur
of stalactites weeping
   and mournful sounds her own voice
      made in the void...

against this improbable trio's drone
  her thoughts, melancholy
    colorless and without scent
blazed out of control
  for her cold hands
    could touch only herself
and she could not see her shadow
  on the wall, her body longing
    to lean in some
direction, toward someone,
  life's lyric having
    neither lilt nor light
so that when she rose
  into luminous day like a flower
    bursting its unbearable bud
she could think only to exclaim:
  "At last! Smells,
    vegetation, brouhaha!"

Watermark

From the opposite bank her eyes followed
the line left by flood seven years before

in its fullness, high point of the river's
passion--like an indelible calling card.

She could trace the path they made together
from the high road, a muddle of footsteps

down to the water's edge, mashed grass and weeds
and hard molded clay. How he taught her

to fish: First bait, then cast, then slow reeling
in of trout. She absorbed the lesson well

and landed a big one, bringing it to
the surface grandly, the hook deep within

in that dark place she could feel in her bones
where hurt persists. And the brilliant water

streaming off like tubes attaching him
to life, how his startled eye penetrated

hers, and all the royal rainbow of him,
his stark yellow lip unfurled, and both

of them learning how the river always
leaves its watermark, high point of its passion.

The Mystery of Picasso
    ...a film

On the big screen
the master, boyish,
puts on an act
doodling for the camera.

His brush loiters, tentative,
lines expanding slowly
to curves, rows of daft
kisses. How he overdoes it!

Then...light
soft colors, cool
Parisian loveliness.
But he will have none of it,

names his ease "courting danger"
smears over mere lucidity
until, out of battered beauty
mysterious grotesqueries

emerge. And with a brush
dipped in Spain's agony
he brands neutral canvas
with Franco's legacy: Guernica.

Snowflakes

You had barely left the room
when the snow came down.
I saw snowflakes
through the window
dipping and soaring
like feathers.
I thought
this must be love
that makes snowflakes
tremble and change course,
fly upwards instead of sinking
to the ground.
You said such phenomena
have rational explanations,
something about
air shafts and up drafts.
But I could scarcely
hear your words
as my heart fluttered irrationally.
And I vowed
when next it snowed
to take you in my arms
and prove you wrong.

Hanging On

Hopper's etching shows
two children digging
near the blind brick wall
of an old house,
motionless in the wan translucent light
at the edge of nowhere.

I remember a house
just off the Turnpike near Secaucus,
a plain flat space where pig farms
once flourished and fed great cities.
Half the house was torn away,
half the roof jutted into dreamspace
at an acute angle
against a horizon that belched soot.

It reminds me of another old house
from a poem we memorized in sixth grade
that went: "Whenever I go to Suffern
along the Erie track,
I go by a farmhouse
with its shingles broken and black.

Hopper's house,
the Turnpike house,
the abandoned farmhouse on the road to Suffern -
for all I know all three are waiting still
though probably shoved out of the way
like the people who once lived there,
who'd be in an old folks home by now
hanging on, letting go slowly,
in their own good time.

String Quartet

After the long stillness of summer
the sound of violins:
Like trees the players,
planted firmly
in prepared ground
in a fertile circle
raise their arms
embrace the swelling shapes of music
and strike the downbeat.
They bend toward each other
like tree tops in the wind
pouring harmonies into the air.
The air whispers
stirs the boughs
and in the long climax of fortissimo
woos without words,
past understanding.

Playing the Recorder

Foolish to flaunt an instrument too slight
for weightier sonorities. A mere
twenty-seven notes in a narrow range
assembled like acrobats on a pyramid.

I often wonder why we struggle through
Holberne and Haydn, plug away at fresh
approaches to a masterpiece like "Hark
the Herald Angels Sing" to lighten up

the sullen holidays for the nursing home
inmates who have ceased harking to angels,
light-hearted or not. Yet I go on practicing
my alto, learning to come in at just

the right moment, striving for a perfect
rainbow of tones to get to the point
where my solo G is followed by a
B natural, and it is so beautiful
I could weep.

A Matter of Faith

At Chichen Itza, after climbing to the top
of the great pyramid, afloat, unanchored,
and part of infinite space, I could see

the Mayan ball court in the near distance.
Beyond that the murky green senote where,
they say humans were also sacrificed.

Meaning the Mayan maidens who long ago
met their watery fate in the menacing pool,
a monument to faith. Yet I lost courage

there, fearing to take the first step down
the rock face I could not see but must count
upon. Certainly not what I was after.

I thought of those who were urged to faith
as salve for fear: heroes of the ball court
game whose mad reward was Paradise and glory.

Sweet Isaac and father Abraham, whose
dagger would outshine the sacrifice. And
old Ramses, about to enter the dark

unknown, metal mirrors shining on his
royal face, wives and worldly goods, wealth
untold to share the final voyage. So,

marveling at their sturdiness of faith,
the promised afterlife, the all-too-pat
solution to their fear of the awful dark

I faltered there at the edge of the abyss,
knowing it hardly mattered, for the fateful
step must be taken, whatever came after.

Saturdays in September

Kurasowa's Dream is playing at the movies
but I can't tear myself away
from the dreams being played out
on the field below
where the littlest ones arrive at eight
and traffic soon grows out of hand
as cars pull in and out discharging small figures in orange
or green or navy blue
with shoulders padded and helmets ready.
Parents stream downhill
trailing lawn chairs and ice chests,
keeping their misgivings to themselves
while gladiators run round the field,
legs churning. too young
for dignity and strut,
and miniature cheer leaders,
legs like sticks, stand ready to go off
like Roman candles.

Saturday Matinee

In the fifteen minutes between
your arrival and the opening
notes of the prologue to Traviata
we exchange news of the weather,
the newlyweds' chances for
happiness, and the latest
illnesses and deaths.
We concur on candidates
for the coming election,
congratulate ourselves
on the state of our health,
and give a brief report
on the progress of our work.
We snap photos in the few minutes
before you run to catch your bus
while scheduling our next rendezvous,
agreeing that true friendship
is no light matter.

Elm

I watch
the giant elm
through all seasons
wonder
how dare
the fitful wind
challenge
an old tree
whose leaves
a peaceful green
its shape
so smooth
its branches
a giant fan.
So calm
though
when it storms
it goes
into action
like all
great fighters
reminding me
of Ali's grace
and Dempsey's skill
a winner.

Windows

Think of a series of windows.
The smallest
at the back
frames your mother and father
in a time before time began.

They are standing
in a store window
helping strangers
to newspapers or cigarettes

and they are waving at you.

It is dark.
You can see a glimmer
of subway train
the old El that unravels
above the street.

It fills your night
with muffled rumbles.

You can hear the soft groan
of engines braking,
see passengers getting
on and off

and then disappearing into darkness…

They are reaching for you.
You can almost feel their fingers
as you search the shadows
and try to keep them in focus.

You remember the many windows
you have waved from,

the El tracks
that have gone underground

and when the nights
are empty and mute
you think of the first
window and the long train
and the lights that flicker
and go out.

A Law of Nature

Mother practiced that high art,
the giving of life.

When a clock stopped
she would turn it face down
search the secret places
of its soul.

She would spread the parts before her
fit them together 'til they meshed.
And when she wound the stem
a steady beat began.

It was like a law of nature,
something in her in tune with
a rationality within the clock
that called home its brood
and made it breathe.

Like gravity
her pull was irresistible.

Woman on the Beach

You'd see her walking the shore
at twilight, feet cushioned
in the soft sand, sea spray pungent.
Rembrandt might have painted her
soft cushions of loving flesh.
He'd lay the paint on lush and dense
reveal her firm and thick as history
the story in her image
enigmatic and restless.
You'd see the light slanting
from sky to rock to shore
and puzzle what it all meant,
like the burghers of Calais.

Legacy

Out of an old photo, faded with age,
my grandmother smiles at me
younger than memory yet primed
to fear, persistence of pogroms,
five children huddled in the rough safety
of steerage and braced to meet the test
at Ellis Island
(one left behind for Babi Yar).

A mother and daughter
exiled and of exiles born,
she stands mild before her small shop window,
her bazaar in Damascus,
her tent on the road to the Indies,
her Mediterranean trader's stall.

Such pride, her name engraved on plate glass,
cropped hair shining free.
She submits to no sad melodies
no widow's black
nor plies a needle
between prayer and candle light.

From having to pick up the pieces
and start again, you get in the habit.
The impulse is to live in the world as it is,
and go on.

Her legacy:
a survivor's smile
and four thousand years of history.

My Mother's Ghost

"Ghosts of ice lurk in water that had been frozen..."

I must be one of the antibodies
Linus Pauling spoke of long ago
and she the protein I wrapped myself
around, so that we were nearly
identical, a chain folding on itself

I walk the way she walked and speak the way
she spoke. I hear her singing songs older
than I am, so that a thread of memory
traces a familiar tone back to her,
the folding and unfolding of wave

and particle I name quantum, a nimbus
luminous and subterranean, lingering
and ghostly and elusive, like a vague
recollection of a former crystalline state,
the hint of ice that lurks in water.

June Walk

When The South Bronx was the last stop
on the El and all the buildings were new
I would watch from the apartment stoop,
my mother calling me to supper from two
flights up, as everyone's father climbed
uphill from the station at twilight,
past the fruit stand and the live chicken
market, only stopping at the candy store
for a paper before mounting to the first
or fifth floor of their cold water flats
where the smells of supper met them
in the hallway.

When the new neighborhood park was the place
we all went for the annual June Walk
and the innocence of hard boiled eggs,
slabs of bread and fresh hard rolls
still warm from paper bags.

When four-year olds were dressed
in crepe paper facsimiles of bridal
gowns and kewpie dolls flourished bouquets
of prickly pink roses, everyone's family
stood around the beribboned canopy
self-conscious with having brought it all off.

That was when the South Bronx was suburbia,
when small children were rewarded with the fruits
of the tropics, one orange apiece,
just for being there, and homemade softballs
hit the dirt, and checker players concentrated,
the men's pinochle game reserved for later,
and the annual June Walk was the neighborhood's
reward to itself for having made it that far.

Souvenirs

Old associations seem to matter
less and less.
The clear blue bottle on the window sill
no longer makes me long
for the ocean at Capri
the Mediterranean light
the blue water.
It hardly matters now
that the muscled fisherman
who ploughed the waves
had shoulders like the hero
of an old movie, with a rose tattoo.
Lately, I prefer morning haze that dulls the trees
before the sun burns through
like chrysanthemums fading into bronze.
Blueness stays.

Letter to an Old Friend

In the manner of Tu Fu

The sun came out briefly today
though an unexpected chill
made me sneeze.
I have lost three friends
and miss them.
I went from doctor to doctor
seeking relief
from the stiffness in my feet.

But I am glad to say the pain
is almost gone
and I have resumed my daily walk.
I find comfort in poetry
and sometimes take solace
in a glass of wine, though
not too often lest it disturb
my digestion.
My friends note that my hair
has not turned white,
and do not refer to the stiffness
of my step.

I look forward to camping out
this summer and soaking
in the water of the lake.

Taking one day at a time
you could even say I'm thriving.